True

Rosa Labordé

True
first published 2016 by
Scirocco Drama
An imprint of J. Gordon Shillingford Publishing Inc.
© 2016 Rosa Labordé

Scirocco Drama Editor: Glenda MacFarlane
Cover design by Terry Gallagher/Doowah Design
Author photo by Max Telzerow
Printed and bound in Canada on 100% post-consumer recycled paper.

We acknowledge the financial support of the Manitoba Arts Council and The Canada
Council for the Arts for our publishing program.

Production inquiries should be addressed to:
Playwrights Guild of Canada
401 Richmond Street West, Suite 350
Toronto, Ontario
M5V 3A8
Telephone: 416-703-0201
Fax: 416-703-0059
orders@playwrightsguild.ca

Library and Archives Canada Cataloguing in Publication

Laborde, Rosa, author
    True / Rosa Labordé.

A play.
ISBN 978-1-927922-25-5 (paperback)

    I. Title.

PS8623.A264T78 2016   C812'.6   C2016-906472-7

J. Gordon Shillingford Publishing
P.O. Box 86, RPO Corydon Avenue, Winnipeg, MB Canada R3M 3S3

Dedicated to the memory of J. Gordon Shillingford

A champion of artists

A passionate publisher

We are forever grateful

"Nothing will come of nothing."
— *King Lear*

Rosa Labordé

Rosa Labordé has been nominated for the Governor General's Literary Award, the Broadway World Toronto Award and the Dora Mavor Moore award for her plays as well as receiving the K.M. Hunter Artist's award for theatre. Plays include: *The Source, Sugar, Leo, Hush, Like Wolves* and *Marine Life*. Rosa is Playwright-in-Residence at the Tarragon Theatre and Aluna Theatre. She is a graduate of The Oxford School of Drama and The Canadian Film Centre and divides her time between acting and writing for theatre, television and film.

The playwright wishes to thank: Aephraim Steinberg from the University of Toronto's Physics Department for consulting on the probabilities of living in a multiverse, as well as Doctor David Tal from St. Joseph's Hospital for his expertise on dementia and Alzheimer's.

Production History

True was first presented at Citizenry Café in Toronto as a co-production between Criminal Theatre and Aluna Theatre in July 2014 for Toronto's Fringe Festival, and after a sold-out run was remounted in the same site-specific venue in September 2014. The cast was as follows:

Roy ....Layne Coleman

Cece .... Ingrid Rae Doucet

Marie ....Sabrina Grdevich

Anita ....Shannon Taylor

Franco .... Scott McCord

Directed by: Rosa Labordé
Designed by: Trevor Schwellnus
Sound Design by: Thomas Ryder Payne
Costume Design by: Lindsay Walker
Stage Managed by: Robin Munro

The development of this play would not have been possible without the generous support of: Scott McCord, Buddies in Bad Times Theatre and Charissa Wilcox, Tarragon Theatre, Tara Nicodemo, Clementine Fields, Marvin Schwartz, Maurice Doucet, Toni Silberman, Susan Krongold, Nisa and Matthew Diamond, Alda Neves, Susan Bowman, Tammy Taylor, Edna Khubyar and Edna Talent Management, James Sedgeworth and Helen Alto, Richard Lee, Aleyah Solomon and Tamara Vuckovic.

Characters

Roy .... A man losing his memory
Anita .... The youngest
Marie .... The middle
Cece... The eldest
Franco .... Marie's husband, a musician

Setting

Real time. And then not.

A Note About the Text

A sentence without a period indicates
a thought that hasn't

A / indicates overlapping dialogue.

A ... on its own indicates a character making
some kind of statement without words.

Playwright's Note

What is a memory other than a story we tell ourselves about the past...

But if memory is subjective, who's to say the story is true...

And if we change the story, what does that mean for our future...

A piano.

A pitcher of water and glasses.

An ikebana flower arrangement. Nearly complete.

As the audience enters FRANCO plays the piano.

Classical. Chopin. He's excellent.

He takes his time. He riffs.

Eventually he changes tracks and starts to play INXS.

FRANCO: *...I was standing, you were there, two worlds collided and they could never ever tear us apart...*

MARIE: I hate. That fucking. Song.

    FRANCO stops playing. MARIE comes in.

We should really be having spaghetti. That was her favourite meal. But whatever. Corn tortillas, avocados, tomatoes—should we write this down? Onions. Will you remember? Lemons. What's wrong?

FRANCO: Nothing.

MARIE: Oh. Okay.

FRANCO: What.

MARIE: You're doing the sad face.

FRANCO: Oh, well, I'm sorry for my face.

MARIE:	I just don't like that song.
FRANCO:	You didn't have to be so shitty about it.
MARIE:	Oh my god, I wasn't, I just, I don't want you to play it. Not today.
FRANCO:	Should we go?
MARIE:	Well now I fucking feel bad.
FRANCO:	Well.

Beat.

FRANCO:	This is what Len was talking about.
MARIE:	…
FRANCO:	We should try the…
MARIE:	Oh no, not the…
FRANCO:	Len said that we have to seize these opportunities to forge a new pathway
MARIE:	Oh god. Okay okay okay. Fine. Give me a do-over.
FRANCO:	You want a do-over?
MARIE:	Yeah, let's start over.
FRANCO:	You can't just do it for me you have to do it for
MARIE:	I'm doing it!

She starts to walk out.

FRANCO:	Hang on hang on. Let's clear the energy.
MARIE:	Do we have to?

FRANCO does an elaborate energy-clearing move. There may be breath and sound.

FRANCO:	All right. Go back.

She goes. He plays the piano. Gets back into the song.

FRANCO: *...two worlds collided and they could never ever tear us apart —*

After a good moment, MARIE returns.

MARIE: ...oh, honey, wow, your playing is so beautiful.

FRANCO: Thanks, darling.

MARIE: But you know what?

FRANCO: What?

MARIE: I've never really been a fan of that song.

FRANCO: No?

MARIE: Would you be offended if I asked you to never ever play it again?

FRANCO: Not at all. Done.

MARIE: Thank you.

FRANCO: No, thank *you*, for asking so nicely.

MARIE: Thank you for letting me.

FRANCO: Thank you for trying. See? This is nice, right?

MARIE: Yeah.

FRANCO: Yeah?

MARIE: You were right. I could have been more

FRANCO: No no no. That didn't even happen.—We should go.

MARIE: 'kay.

They go. Time passes. Too much maybe.

ROY enters. He wears a suit jacket over pajamas.

ROY: ...hm... is this? Uh? Hello? Is this the...?

He looks at a crumpled piece of paper in his hand.

ANITA enters.

ANITA: We're closed now, actually. The door should have been locked—they have a habit of forgetting to

ROY: Hi.

ANITA: ...how did you...

ROY: This is the place.

ANITA: What are you doing here...

ROY: Your hair is darker.

ANITA: Um... you should... you should probably... go.

ROY: Who plays the piano?

ANITA: ...Roy

ROY: I play the piano?

ANITA: Roy as in 'Roy, go now' not 'Roy plays the piano'.

ROY: Roy doesn't play the piano?

ANITA: No. Or I don't know. Do you?

ROY: Your hair is darker. With your eyes it's so

ANITA: You're in pajamas.

ROY notices his pajamas. As though for the first time.

ROY: You love pajamas. You used to wear them all day. You'd say, 'I've got my cozies on.'

ANITA: That was Marie.

ROY: Marie.

ANITA: Marie won't want to see you, so you should probably

ROY: I'm quite thirsty—do you mind if I...? May I have a drop of that water?

ANITA: Please, Dad

ROY: Dad. Words they—like a pierce. Exquisite. And you

ANITA: ...are you... crying?

ROY: I'm fine. Just; Dad. Your hair is darker.

ANITA: I'm older. I think that just happens.

ROY: You had more blonde, but now

ANITA: It's dull?

ROY: No it's. You're so... you're...

ANITA: You're in pajamas. Do you just, out in the streets, wear

ROY: Who plays the piano?

ANITA: Marie's husband.

ROY: Marie's...?

ANITA: Yes.

ROY: Can I have some water?

ANITA: Sure. Wait. No. You can't.

ROY: All right. I'll just. It was nice to

ANITA: ...wait. I have a... shirt. I think it would fit you if you... we could trade the pajama top for the... come, let me take your jacket.

ROY: That's all right.

ANITA: No it's nothing. I have one that should fit.

              She finds him a shirt.

ANITA: Yes. Here.

ROY: Oh, that is so

ANITA: Do you think it's

ROY: Fantastic

ANITA: I designed it

ROY: You? Oh, Anita, it's

ANITA: I'm glad you like it

ROY: I do

ANITA: Hand me your jacket

              He gives her the piece of paper he's been holding.

              Then takes off his jacket and hands it to her. She gives him the shirt.

ROY: You designed this... it's so... yes

              He starts to change. ANITA turns to give him privacy. Her cell phone rings.

ANITA: (*into phone*) I can't talk—what? No. No, I told you already I won't eat spaghetti. No Italian food. I won't. Because! Mexican we said.

              She turns to ROY. He is wearing the new shirt and only his boxer shorts.

              I gotta go.

              She hangs up.

              Well, the shirt fits. It suits you, actually. But I'm not sure I have pants that fit, so you might want to put your pajama bottoms back on.

CECE enters holding fresh cut flowers.

She sees ROY and the flowers fall to the floor.

ROY: Celeste. You dropped your flowers. Celeste.

ANITA: She goes by Cece now. It's been years.

ROY: Years?

ANITA: He just showed up. With this.

She gives CECE the paper.

ROY collects the flowers off the ground.

ROY: I think that's all of them. Except for the little sticks.

ANITA: She uses those.

ROY: The sticks?

ANITA: She's an ikebana flower arranger.

ROY: A what?

ANITA: The Japanese art of flower arrangement.

ROY: Oh. Here.

CECE takes the flowers and adds them to her unfinished arrangement, ignoring ROY.

           Celeste is so quiet.

ANITA: Cece.

ROY: Cece. Sorry. Cece is so quiet.

ANITA: Uh, yeah… she's quiet when she's arranging. It's very spiritual—Zen almost

ROY: Zen? Like meditation, Celeste? I mean, Cece. Like meditation, Cece? Like that? Cece?

CECE: Wh-what are you d-d-doing here?

ROY: Are you all right?

CECE: Wh-when d-did you g-get here?

ROY: Why are you talking like that?

CECE: Wh-what?

ROY: Your speech, it's so

ANITA: Dad

ROY: broken.

CECE: It's a n-n-neurogenic s-s-stutter

ROY: How did you get it?

ANITA: Dad

CECE: T-trauma t-to the head.

ROY: Can't you fix it?

CECE: N-no.

ROY: There must be something you could do

CECE: No.

ROY: Are you sure?

CECE: Some things are d-done that c-c-can't be undone.

ROY: I'm sorry. Does it

ANITA: Dad

ROY: Does it hurt?

CECE: No.

ROY: Has it been a long time?

CECE: ...yes.

ROY:	I'm so sorry. If I'd known I'd have… I don't know. Something.
CECE:	…well…
ROY:	Who plays the piano?
ANITA:	…Marie's husband?
ROY:	Marie's married?
ANITA:	Yes.
ROY:	That's. Well. Time.
ANITA:	Dad, you can't smoke in here.
ROY:	Oh, sorry
ANITA:	Go outside if you have to smoke.
ROY:	Of course
ANITA:	You shouldn't be smoking at all, not at your
ROY:	I know, it's—sorry
MARIE:	*(OS)* They were out of avocados!
ANITA:	Go! Smoke out back. Now.

He goes. MARIE and FRANCO enter.

MARIE:	They were completely out of avocados and you can't make Mexican without avocados so we *had* to go with spaghetti. I'm sorry, Anita. I tried
ANITA:	We're not having spaghetti
MARIE:	Tell her, Franco
FRANCO:	Spaghetti
MARIE:	I just couldn't remember why you don't eat it—it's not an allergy /

FRANCO:	/It's not an allergy?/
MARIE:	/so I call you, but
ANITA:	You know why
MARIE:	See, there's a story isn't there?
ANITA:	You have to start locking the door
MARIE:	Banita, relax
FRANCO:	Yeah, Banita
ANITA:	Anita
MARIE:	Banita, Baby Anita, which you are
ANITA:	Anyone could just walk in
MARIE:	She was in Italy—Rome! At the famous fountain— what's it...?
CECE:	T-Trevi
MARIE:	Trevi! This is a great story.
ANITA:	Which part? The part where I was sexually assaulted by a fountain?
MARIE:	You weren't sexually/ assaulted
ANITA:	/He pulled out his
MARIE:	Some lonely flasher—you were the highlight of his life
FRANCO:	It's a crime, flashing
ANITA:	Not in Italy
MARIE:	So...
CECE:	She's at the f-f-fountain and she asks for d-d-directions and instead of d-d-directions this guy pulls out his sch-schlong—happy?

FRANCO:	That's why you don't eat spaghetti?
ANITA:	No! It was when I came back and told my friends and it turned out half the girls I knew had been flashed on holiday in Rome.
FRANCO:	Gross
MARIE:	That's what she said
CECE:	At the c-consulate
FRANCO:	The consulate?
MARIE:	She goes to the fucking consulate!
ANITA:	Oh my god
FRANCO:	What'd they say?
ANITA:	You're young and pretty it's to be expected
CECE:	M-Marie, we have to t-tell you
MARIE:	Condoning. Can you believe…?
FRANCO:	You should have complained. Gone higher up.
ANITA:	To who? The church of touching little boys?
FRANCO:	So that's why you don't eat Italian food?
ANITA:	Yeah
FRANCO:	That's the stupidest thing I've ever heard.
ANITA:	Okay, well, I didn't ask for your opinion, so
FRANCO:	What does that even do?
ANITA:	It's a statement.
FRANCO:	To who?
ANITA:	Italy.

FRANCO: I don't think Italy knows you're not eating pasta

ANITA: And I don't buy Italian shoes so: the economy? I'm not supporting it.

FRANCO: I did not realize you were responsible for Italia's economic crisis until right now

ANITA: I didn't even want to tell this story

FRANCO: But you do every day/

ANITA: /I don't/

FRANCO: /every time you don't order pizza because of a penis you once saw you reinforce it—something that happened, what, over ten years ago, defines your existence now?

ANITA: It doesn't define

FRANCO: Let it go

CECE: F-Franco

FRANCO: I'm serious, let that shit go

ANITA: But it happened.

FRANCO: Unhappen it.

ANITA: What does that even mean

FRANCO: You're at the fountain but this time you get directions

ANITA: He pulled out his penis!

FRANCO: Or he was eating an Italian sausage for lunch—it doesn't matter anymore because you and me, we're standing at the Trevi fountain, right now—I'll be the guy, you be you, ask me for directions, I promise not to pull out my—okay: go!

CECE: No, this isn't a g-g-good time to

FRANCO: It's the perfect time. Go!

ANITA: What?

FRANCO: The reenactment.

MARIE: We do this.

FRANCO: It works.

MARIE: It's like a do-over.

ANITA: No. No. I am not doing one of the exercises you do with your weirdo couples' counselor.

FRANCO: Len is not weird!

MARIE: Len is a little weird.

ANITA: I can't do this right now

CECE: There's something we have t-t-to t-t-tell you

FRANCO: Is it weird to choose a better life? Len says every road not taken is another potential life path, another dimension—like multiverse theory; daughter universes—and if we just make a different choice we can access that other universe

ANITA: Franco, I don't know what the fuck you're talking about right now but

FRANCO: I'm talking about cracking open your concept of reality and knowing you have the power to change it. Like that day at the fountain, you asked for directions and got a... map!

MARIE: And we can eat spaghetti. It's like a cosmic fucking do-over.

FRANCO: Hey, some guy's outside our window.

MARIE: Who's outside our

ANITA: He just showed up

MARIE: No

ANITA: I tried to make him go but he

CECE: No you d-didn't

MARIE: No no no

FRANCO: Who is that?

MARIE: He needs to go now

FRANCO: Who is that?

CECE: R-Roy

FRANCO: That's Roy?

ANITA: He came with this letter—he's not in a good—I just gave him a shirt

MARIE: You gave him a shirt?

ANITA: He was wearing pajamas

MARIE: Who cares? I don't care

ANITA: Would you just read this? Please.

MARIE: Dear Anita—it's not even to me, it's not for me, I don't want to read

ANITA: Please

MARIE: *You and your sisters not easy to track down. We found out about clothing sale from Facebook*—Facebook?

ANITA: I had to advertise—how else would people know where to

MARIE: They walk by

ANITA: It's the twenty-first century

MARIE: Did you put it anywhere else?

ANITA: Twitter.

MARIE: Banita!

ANITA: Oh god, sorry, okay, I'm sorry I tweet

MARIE: That's not the—fuck, fine, I don't care—twit, twitter, tweet all you like; be a flock of wild birds for all I care, just get him out of here.

ANITA: Me? It's not just me—that letter is for all of us, it says me and my sisters

MARIE: It's addressed to you from... who wrote this? 'A friend'? Oh this is nice; *to abandon one's father is greatest sin of all, your father has Alzheimer's, he can no longer care for himself. In case like this responsibility is yours and sisters*—the fuck it is, can you believe this? It's not even proper English.

ROY: Hello.

ANITA: Go smoke

ROY: I just finished

ANITA: Have another. Go. Now.

ROY: All right.

MARIE: Wrong door, Banita.

ANITA: I'm just giving us a minute to figure out

MARIE: There's nothing to figure out

CECE: Maybe we should t-t-talk about this m-more calmly

MARIE: How are you calm? How are you calm? You knew he was out there? This whole time, Cece, and you didn't even tell me?

CECE: I was t-trying to t-tell you—!

MARIE: And today, on the anniversary of Mom's—of all the days to

ANITA:	I don't think he knows what day it is, Marie, he's not the same, his mind is
MARIE:	I don't care, just make him go.
ANITA:	…I can't.
MARIE:	You can't.
ANITA:	No. Not just like that. Not in his
MARIE:	Fine. Cece?
CECE:	I, I, please d-d-don't ask *me* to
MARIE:	Well, I don't want to talk to him so, Franco, can you please
FRANCO:	Wha…?

He does an energy-clearing move.

Woo! The energy in here is… yeah, and sometimes you just gotta shift the atmosphere—let's do this, do it with me, everyone; clean the slate, new perspective—

He tries to pull them into a move.

MARIE:	Just get him out.
FRANCO:	I, uh, I think my answer is—and not that I don't wanna do whatever makes you happy because that's my, you know, that's our pledge, to make each other… which is so great—and you do, so thank you for my happiness but my gut is saying that I should stay out of the, so, no.
MARIE:	Fine. I'll do it.
FRANCO:	Okay.
MARIE:	Hey. Roy.
ROY:	Oh. Hello.

MARIE:	Hi.
ROY:	Hello.
MARIE:	Hi.
ROY:	Hello.
MARIE:	How's your cigarette?
ROY:	You look just like your
MARIE:	Yeah, I know. Put it out.
ROY:	Sure.
MARIE:	...it's time to go now.
ROY:	Is it?
MARIE:	It is.
ROY:	I don't have a watch.
MARIE:	Or pants.
ROY:	You used to wear pajamas all day. You'd say, 'I've got my cozies on'!
MARIE:	Memory lane. That's sweet.
ROY:	You'd climb into my arms and say, 'I'm wearing my cozies in the cozy.'
MARIE:	That was a long time ago.
ROY:	Climb in.
MARIE:	No.
ROY:	I could still hold you.
MARIE:	I don't think so.
ROY:	My little girl.

MARIE: Fuck

ANITA: Told you

ROY: Karate flowers!

MARIE: What?

ANITA: I think he means ikebana.

ROY: Aren't they just so… yes.

MARIE: He's on something.

ANITA: What, like drugs?

FRANCO: Some kind of anti-anxiety

MARIE: Right?

FRANCO: Yeah.

ROY: Hello.

FRANCO: Hi there. I'm Franco. So nice to finally meet you.

MARIE: Is it?

ROY: Franco died.

FRANCO: Probably a different Franco.

ROY: What Franco did to Spain was

FRANCO: That was a totally different Franco. I'm not even Spanish. Half Portuguese. My mother's from Portugal.

ROY: Who are you?

FRANCO: Franco.

ROY: …where are my pants? What did you do to my pants!?

FRANCO: I—no—I didn't

ROY:	You stole my pants!
FRANCO:	I didn't.
ROY:	Louise!
CECE:	Louise isn't
ROY:	Louise!
MARIE:	Make him stop.
FRANCO:	Did he have anything on him? Pills or…?
ANITA:	I'll check.
ROY:	Where am I? Louise!
MARIE:	Roy
ROY:	Oh thank god. Louise.
MARIE:	I'm not
ROY:	Louise.
MARIE:	Oh no, don't hug me
ROY:	Qu'est ce qui ce passe?
MARIE:	No. Step back.
ROY:	I'm sorry. It didn't mean anything.
MARIE:	Just step back.
ROY:	I told you before. She's no one to me.
MARIE:	What?
ROY:	I love you and I'm sorry.
MARIE:	Get him away from me.
FRANCO:	Roy. I'm just gonna have you step back, buddy.

ROY: Don't touch me!

CECE: Dad. Stop.

ROY: Our fighting is making the girls nervous, Louise.

MARIE: Get away from me.

ROY: I'm your husband. Don't you dare push me back like that! Ever!

MARIE: There you are. You may have fooled them but you can't fool me. I know what you are.

ROY: Can you blame me for wanting a woman with just a little bit of class?

MARIE: Why don't you have another drink, you fuck

ROY: There's your mouth, you dirty little

MARIE: You're disgusting

ROY: En Francais, Petit Chou

                     MARIE starts hitting him.

MARIE: Tu veux que je te parle en Francais, Papa, c'est ça que tu veux

ANITA: Oh shit.

ROY: Ow, Marie, ow.

CECE: M-M-Marie stop.

FRANCO: Okay okay, come on. Come here. Come on.

ANITA: Dad, stand up.

MARIE: I told you

FRANCO: I'm sorry

MARIE: Put on some pants, for god's sake. Where are his pants?

ANITA: He had—it doesn't matter—here, put your pajama pants back on okay, Dad? Dad?

ROY: Okay.

MARIE: I need some air.

CECE: I'll c-c-come.

ANITA: Hang on. Me too.

ROY: Can I come?

ANITA: Not now.

ROY: What's wrong?

ANITA: Watch him, okay? These pills were in his pocket.

FRANCO: Uh.

ROY: Is Marie all right?

              The sisters go outside.

ROY: Is Marie all right?

FRANCO: Hey, do you wanna make guacamole?

ROY: No.

FRANCO: Come on, let's make guacamole.

ROY: I've never done that before.

FRANCO: No?

ROY: Or have I?

FRANCO: Let's find out.

ROY: Who are you?

FRANCO: Fr… ank.

ROY: Frank?

FRANCO:	Marie's... husband.
ROY:	Marie got married?
FRANCO:	Uh huh. All right. We've got avocados, onions, tomatoes
ROY:	When?
FRANCO:	A year and a half ago. How are you with a knife? Actually, no, let's not, do that.
ROY:	Where?
FRANCO:	What?
ROY:	Did you get married.
FRANCO:	Mejico.
ROY:	Mexico?
FRANCO:	We love the food. Guacamole is Mexican.
ROY:	In a church?
FRANCO:	On a beach.
ROY:	Who was there?
FRANCO:	Cece, Anita, my brother, my mom—I mean, it was—it was really small. I'll cut the onion, you mash the avocado, okay? I'll just scoop out the
ROY:	Who gave her away?
FRANCO:	There we go
ROY:	Who gave her away?
FRANCO:	Here's a fork. No. Here's a spoon. You can mash it with a spoon.
ROY:	Who gave her away?

FRANCO: You know, we didn't really, uh, it was more of a mutual coming together thing.

ROY: No one gave her away?

FRANCO: Not really. Just mash it. We want it really mashed.

ROY: Did anyone give her away?

FRANCO: Cece and Anita walked her—either side of her—it was beautiful.

ROY: That sounds…

FRANCO: Is that the onions or are you…

ROY: I'm fine

FRANCO: This is why it's better just to mash the avocados. No talking. More mashing.

ROY: I'm mashing.

FRANCO: It's trickier with a spoon, but

ROY: I should have given her away.

FRANCO: Try not to cry in the guacamole—the emotion you cook with ends up in the food

ROY: My parents weren't at my wedding either. She wasn't what they wanted for me, so. They were very, you know, they had an idea of who I was, some vague notion to do with class or intellect, who knows, just an idea she didn't… correspond to. They threatened not to come but I didn't think they meant it, I thought for sure they'd show up and I waited, stupid. We started an hour and a half late because I was sure they would—but they never, so. My wedding night I sat in that… you know, the tiny pool, the tiny pool where the water sprays on you

FRANCO: The bathtub?

ROY: The tub in our hotel room, in my tux with the shower on, water blasting down on me, a bottle of rum in my hand and Louise in my lap singing French songs while I cried.

FRANCO: I think that's good for the avocado—we don't want to puree it, just

ROY: Did she cry? On her wedding night?

FRANCO: I have an idea. It's this thing I do, totally shifts the energy when you get stuck in a pattern of—we just—and it can be personal to you, you know, you just change your posture—but make a move, like a dramatic kind of, yeah, move—and a sound, like a big HAI-YAH!

ROY: Ah.

FRANCO: Do it with me. HAI-YAH!

ROY: Hai-yahhh...

FRANCO: Nice. Now make it your own. Whatever you want. Whatever comes out of you. Movement and sound. Shake everything off. Come on.

ROY: Uh...

FRANCO: Whatever. BOOM.

ROY: BOOM. Ha ha.

FRANCO: Yeah. Great. Doesn't that feel...? Yeah...?

ROY: Who plays the piano?

FRANCO: I do.

ROY: Oh that's... I love the piano. You're so lucky you can play... you—who are you?

FRANCO: Frank. When you take these pills do you take one or two?

ROY: …two?

FRANCO takes two pills and gives them to ROY.

Thank you.

FRANCO gives him some water. ROY takes the pills. Then FRANCO takes a few pills for himself and pops them back. ROY doesn't notice.

Would you play something?

FRANCO: *(swallowing)* Yeah? Sure. What do you want to hear?

ROY: Oh, anything.

FRANCO: All right, I'll play the piano, you squeeze the lemon.

ROY: …is that a euphemism for…

FRANCO: What? No. Just squeeze the lemon. Into the avocado.

ROY: Right.

FRANCO begins to play. He plays throughout.

ROY: Oh, that's… yes. Oh, yeah.

FRANCO: Don't forget the lemon.

ROY: Yes.

FRANCO: Watch for the pips—take them out.

ROY: Is this a piano bar?

FRANCO: It's a cafe.

ROY: It's yours?

FRANCO: Mine and Marie's. Sometimes Anita sells her clothes here.

ROY: I'd like a drink.

FRANCO: Water, pop, coffee, tea. Help yourself.

ROY: No, I'd like a—

FRANCO: There's no booze here. Dry dry dry. Marie and I met in rehab so…

ROY: Oh. Well, I don't think I'm supposed to drink with my medication anyhow.

FRANCO: It's not recommended.

ROY: I have Alzheimer's. Which may have been caused by drinking too much or drinking too little. They can't be sure. A couple of drinks staves it off but a few too many brings it on.

FRANCO: How long?

ROY: Huh?

FRANCO: Have you had it.

ROY: Oh. I can't remember. Get it?

FRANCO: Ha ha. How does it feel?

ROY: What?

FRANCO: Losing your…

ROY: Mind? Is that what I'm losing? Am I going completely

He breaks off and heads to where the girls are.

Where are those girls?

FRANCO: Come away from the window. Give them some space.

ROY: How much space can they need? I haven't seen them in…

FRANCO: …do you remember why…?

ROY: They're lovely these. The Buddhist flowers.

FRANCO: Maybe that's a blessing. People torture themselves
            with memories. I have. I *do*. Less now. I mean, I try
            not to. But still, things I've done I'm not proud of.
            Things done to me. My blood gets hot, my stomach
            tight, I shake—just thinking about it—like it's
            happening all over again. That's why I, you know,
            Boom, change it, shift the energy—don't want to
            reinforce the pathway—the circuit—you know
            what I'm talking about? The neural

ROY: Just play the piano.

FRANCO: Okay.

            FRANCO plays again.

ROY: You play so… yeah, you're very…

FRANCO: I started really young. Child prodigy. *They* thought.
            Any instrument, I could just—so you know,
            competitions, medals, little write-ups in the paper,
            then bands, then drugs, so many drugs and—fuck!
            I could have played in symphonies—not that those
            guys don't do drugs but—shit—Carnegie Hall, you
            know, instead of living on tour buses playing with
            whoever—oh poor me, poor me—I know I have the
            power to change my goddamn thoughts and rewire
            my brain but still I get fuckin' caught

ROY: Why don't you just sing.

FRANCO: A sense of humour. I wouldn't have known that.
            Not based on their Tales-From-The-Crypt version
            of you.

ROY: Tales From The—?

FRANCO: Never mind. Makes sense now—their humour,
            the way they play—of course they got it from
            somewhere.

ROY: Nothing comes from nothing.

FRANCO: Nothing ever did.—But what's it like? Seriously. Are memories just erased? 'Cause I would love that, in a way, selectively—not all, but—how does it feel?

ROY: Questions I don't know the answers to.

FRANCO: Sorry to ask

ROY: No, that's how it feels. Stupid.

FRANCO: Because the answers are just gone?

ROY: Gone.

FRANCO: But sometimes you're all the way in a memory—like you're living it again

ROY: What?

FRANCO: Like you think something is something else

ROY: I don't know—

FRANCO: Like you're here but you're there

ROY: What?

FRANCO: You're in the present and the past at the same time—you're in two places at once—it's like you exist in two dimensions, you know? Hey, what if you're, like, unconsciously trying to fix your memories? You think?

ROY: I don't know what that means. Just play the piano. But songs I can sing. I know songs. I don't forget them.

FRANCO: You got it.

                    FRANCO plays.

ROY: Like that. Yes. I know this. My cherie amour.

FRANCO:	By?
ROY:	Stevie Wonder.
FRANCO:	What about this?
ROY:	Too easy. Everyone knows it.
FRANCO:	Name the artist.
ROY:	Withers. Bill.
FRANCO:	And this…?
ROY:	Al Green.
FRANCO:	This?
ROY:	Beethoven. I can't sing that.
FRANCO:	Sorry. This?
ROY:	What's that…? The Shondells?
FRANCO:	Nice. You're one for one. This?
ROY:	Oh… oh… *time may change me but I can't change time*—Bowie!
FRANCO:	Marie never told me you were so
ROY:	Marie?
FRANCO:	Yeah.
ROY:	She's the spitting image of my…
FRANCO:	I know.
ROY:	Are you married?
FRANCO:	I am. To Marie.
ROY:	Marie's married?
FRANCO:	She is.

ROY: That's. Well. Time.

FRANCO: We got married in Mexico. You don't remember
                this?

ROY: Mexico? It's hot there.

FRANCO: The day of the wedding was very hot.

ROY: Yes. Did I get a sunburn?

FRANCO: Uh. You… wore a hat.

ROY: I did. Yes, I did. Good. Oh no.

FRANCO: What?

ROY: For a second I couldn't remember I'd been there. I
                couldn't remember my own daughter's wedding. I
                was there, wasn't I?

FRANCO: You gave her away.

ROY: Of course I did. Yes. Of course.

FRANCO: It's a good memory. It was a great day.

                The sisters come in.

FRANCO: We made guacamole.

ROY: Did we?

FRANCO: You mashed the avocado.

ROY: I did.

ANITA: I thought there weren't any avocados!

MARIE: Sorry.

FRANCO: You all right?

MARIE: Better.

FRANCO: I'm gonna get the barbecue going. Get the fish on
                there. We're having fish tacos.

ANITA: Mmm.

              He goes outside.

ROY: I like Frank.

MARIE: Franco.

ROY: Frank.

MARIE: Roy, we have a question.

ROY: Roy. Yes.

MARIE: We're just wondering, who wrote the letter?

ROY: What letter?

MARIE: This one in my hand.

ROY: I don't know.

ANITA: It came with you, you brought it

MARIE: Some friend of yours?

ROY: You look just like your

MARIE: Focus on the letter.

ROY: Okay.

MARIE: Do you know what it says?

ROY: No.

MARIE: It says you have Alzheimer's.

ROY: Oh no.

MARIE: Did you know that?

ROY: Who knows what caused it.

MARIE: So you know.

ROY: Did I drink too much or too little…

MARIE: I think we all know the answer to that. Where do you live?

ROY: I forget things.

MARIE: Do you live with your friend?

ROY: My friend?

MARIE: Who wrote this letter.

ROY: Who wrote that letter?

ANITA: Marie, I don't think—

MARIE: We need to know—he's not staying here—who was it?

ROY: Who?

MARIE: Your friend?

ROY: What friend?

MARIE: Your friend who wrote the letter.

ROY: I don't—I don't

MARIE: Look at this letter. Look at it.

ROY: All right.

MARIE: Did a man write this letter?

ROY: Hm.

MARIE: A woman?

ROY: Perhaps.

MARIE: Tall or short?

ROY: ...I don't...

MARIE: Young or old?

ROY: …

MARIE: Young or old?

ROY: What is—how do you define old?

MARIE: Oh for god's sake!

ROY: Young! No. Old!

MARIE: …was it you?

ANITA: What?

MARIE: Did you write this letter, Roy?

ROY: Let me see.

ANITA: Of course he didn't—

MARIE: Did you?

ROY: Uh… sure, yes. Yes! I wrote this letter.

ANITA: You—what?

MARIE: You wrote 'to abandon one's father is greatest sin of all?'

ROY: I don't remember that.

MARIE: No, it wouldn't be very convenient to remember that.

ANITA: You wrote the letter, Dad?

ROY: Banita…

ANITA: Why would you say a friend wrote it if you wrote it?

ROY: I don't know…

MARIE: We couldn't trust him before, we can't trust him now.

ANITA: No. Can you please remember, Dad?

                ROY snaps an elastic band around his wrist.

ANITA: Just try to remember.

                He snaps another.

ROY: Unplug the toaster. *Snap.* Lock the front door. *Snap.* Stay inside past dark. *Snap.* Little girls laughing in the park. Mine. I remember. I'm supposed to pick you up from school. I go to the school. You're not there. Louise is going to kill me. Where are the girls? Where are my little girls? I wake up on a park bench. Why? *Snap.* I don't know. *Snap.* No. *Snap.* What? I can't remember what I'm meant to remember. Then a piece of paper. 'Find the girls'. Clues all over. I write them for myself from myself—the other self who knows who he's writing to and what he's writing about. Instructions to me from me. A mystery novel, a purpose, a meaning, my girls, but then… fear, they hate me, why? *Snap.* I can't remember. *Snap.* The smell of spring and was it always so… birds—fifteen different bird songs in the same cluster—were there always so many? Colours—light—everything is so… you're little, running, playing, blowing bubbles, I'm young, Louise is so… she was always so… and then I'm old, an old man alone in an apartment—which is which? I don't know who wrote that letter but I'm guessing that it was probably me.

MARIE: It *was* you. It was you.

ROY: Probably.

MARIE: Not probably. Yes.

CECE: What d-d-difference does it m-make.

MARIE: He's either helpless or manipulative, that's the

CECE: No. He r-remembers or he d-d-doesn't.

ROY:	What's wrong with your—why are you talking like that?
MARIE:	I can't believe this
ROY:	Your speech. It's so…
ANITA:	Dad.
ROY:	Broken.
MARIE:	That's enough, Roy.
ROY:	Why is it like that?
CECE:	It's a n-neurogenic s-s-stutter.
ROY:	Can't you fix it?
CECE:	N-no.
ANITA:	There's an earpiece she can wear sometimes that helps—
CECE:	B-but it g-g-gives me a h-h-h—
ANITA:	Headache.

FRANCO peeks in.

FRANCO:	Is Roy staying for tacos?
ROY:	Sure!
MARIE:	No.
ANITA:	Yes. You don't get to decide everything.
MARIE:	Go outside for a minute, Roy.
ROY:	I'll have a cigarette.
MARIE:	You do that.

He goes out with FRANCO.

How did he find us, Anita?

ANITA: Facebook.

MARIE: Yeah but don't you need to be friends? I mean, doesn't he have to be your friend to see where you are, what you're doing? Are you friends with him? Have you been friends with him on fucking Facebook?

ANITA: …only for a…

MARIE: You led him here.

ANITA: Not on purpose.

MARIE: Oh my god.

ANITA: He's changed.

MARIE: He lied. He admitted it.

ANITA: All he admitted is he can't remember anything— his mind is

MARIE: I'm not taking care of him. You two can but don't expect me to

ANITA: No one's asking you to

CECE: At least g-get him to a h-hospital

ANITA: Yeah, just give us a second to

MARIE: You shouldn't, though—he didn't take care of you so

ANITA: Would you please just

MARIE: He did the opposite, actually, so

ANITA: We know what you think. Don't bully us into—

MARIE: I'm not bullying—

CECE: Y-you are—

MARIE:	I'm protecting you!
CECE:	N-no.

FRANCO comes in.

FRANCO:	I forgot the lemons.
MARIE:	Am I a bully?
FRANCO:	What?
MARIE:	Am I a bully? Do I bully?
FRANCO:	What do you mean?
MARIE:	Which part of the question didn't you understand?
FRANCO:	Well, in what context?
MARIE:	In any context. Am I a bully?
FRANCO:	I don't know how to answer this.
MARIE:	It's a yes or no question.
FRANCO:	Is it a trick question?
MARIE:	Why would it be a—no—it's just a question. Am I a bully?
FRANCO:	I don't think I should get involved.
MARIE:	I just asked you a simple question.
FRANCO:	Is it, though?
MARIE:	What's the matter with you?
FRANCO:	We bought a lot of lemons. I think I just need one—no, two—no, one—for the fish.
MARIE:	Are you high?
FRANCO:	What.
MARIE:	Look at me.

FRANCO: Not high—no, this isn't high… but I had to look out
            for Roy

MARIE: You didn't

FRANCO: because the label on the bottle was suspicious to me

MARIE: The label on the bottle was suspicious—are you
            insane! Give it to me.

FRANCO: Are you gonna bully me now into

MARIE: I'm not a bully

FRANCO: You have an intensity that I personally find very
            erotic

MARIE: Give me the bottle

FRANCO: Relax—but some might consider it to be

MARIE: Thank you

FRANCO: Bullying.

MARIE: No.

FRANCO: Yeah.

                He goes outside with the lemons.

ANITA: See?

MARIE: What does he know? He's high.

ANITA: Miss it?

MARIE: Of course not.

ANITA: I used to find you huddled under pool tables so off
            your ass you were speaking in tongues

MARIE: That's the past

ANITA: I'd have to carry you home and put you in the
            shower to bring you back

MARIE:	Years ago
ANITA:	I know 'cause I wasn't even old enough to get a drink at the bar. I'd beg them to let me in just so I could get you.
MARIE:	Cece should've come. She's the oldest.
ANITA:	Cece couldn't because…
MARIE:	Why?
ANITA:	Doesn't matter.
CECE:	They m-m-made fun of me.
MARIE:	…sorry.
ANITA:	If Cece—of all of us—is willing to
MARIE:	Cece shouldn't
ANITA:	Cece can do whatever she wants
CECE:	D-don't s-speak for m-me!

MARIE & ANITA: Sorry.

ANITA:	You'll forgive Franco but you can't give Dad one chance
MARIE:	Forgive Franco for what?
ANITA:	He just did drugs
MARIE:	They're prescription pills
ANITA:	You met in rehab!
MARIE:	So?
ANITA:	And isn't that kind of fucked up? I mean, aren't you supposed to, like, not have a relationship for a year when you get sober?

MARIE: Fuck, Banita, *lock the door, don't date drug addicts.* I live on earth. It's a little more complicated than

CECE: Enough!

MARIE: And they're just prescription pills, they're hardly drugs.

ANITA: Sure. Whatever you say, Marie.

            Beat.

MARIE: So, what? We take care of him? After all these years—after everything he did, just open our doors, our hearts, our bank accounts and what? Play happy family? Is that what you want, Cece? Cece, is that what you want? Is it?

CECE: I don't know! I don't—but—slow d-d-down, just calm, p-p-please, you can be just like h-h-h

MARIE: What?

CECE: N-nothing.

MARIE: …I can be just like…? What were you going to say?

CECE: It d-d-doesn't matter.

MARIE: I can't believe you think I'm anything like…

CECE: Marie, just… let's take a b-b-breath to slow d-down and separate p-past from p-present.

MARIE: The past is present. You're living proof of that.

ANITA: Marie!

MARIE: Well!

CECE: …The p-past is only p-present if you never let it go.

            Beat.

ANITA: Irina Semenyuk.

            ANITA is looking at the pill bottle.

CECE: What?

ANITA: On the bottle. Irina Semenyuk.

MARIE: Show me.

ANITA: The label. Look.

MARIE: Irina Semenyuk?

            ROY comes in.

ROY: Frank wants me to help set the table.

MARIE: Whose name is on your pill bottle?

ROY: Huh?

MARIE: Irina Semenyuk.

ROY: Oh, Irina.

MARIE: Is that your girlfriend?

ROY: Ha! No, no. Irina. No.

MARIE: Who is she?

ROY: My doctor.

MARIE: Why's her name on your pills? It should be your name.

ROY: …I don't know…

MARIE: Where does she work?

ROY: What?

MARIE: What hospital do you go to?

ROY: No hospitals!

ANITA: There's a number on the bottle.We could just call—

ROY: No hospitals!

MARIE: Call it.

> *ANITA does. They wait.*

MARIE: So?

ANITA: It's ringing.

MARIE: …Now?

ANITA: It's ringing.

> *Beat.*

            …It's—it's a machine. It's… Irina's housecleaning service?

ROY: She's a doctor. Who cleans.

MARIE: Did your cleaning lady tell you you have Alzheimer's?

ROY: In Kiev she's a doctor, but here… it could take years.

MARIE: Amazing.

ANITA: Did she write this letter?

ROY: Let me see. Oh yes, yes. Irina.

ANITA: I knew he didn't write the letter.

CECE: Why n-no hospitals?

ROY: No. No hospitals. Not since… not since Louise…

MARIE: Since she died?

ROY: Frank asked me to help set the table.

MARIE: Fine. Go ahead.

ROY: For how many? For how many, Marie? One, two, three, four…?

MARIE: Fuck. Five.

ROY: Five. Yes. Good. Five.

            He goes.

ANITA: Thank you

MARIE: Uh huh

ANITA: It'll just give us a little time to figure out

MARIE: Yeah

ANITA: Didn't you miss him? Ever?

MARIE: No. I didn't.

            ROY comes back.

ROY: Frank said to get napkins from the—

MARIE: I'll get them.

            MARIE goes to get napkins.

ROY: And the guacamole. We're having tacos, just like at the wedding.

ANITA: The wedding?

ROY: Marie and Frank's wedding. It was so hot, remember?

ANITA: It was hot, but…

ROY: Mejico

ANITA: You weren't there—

ROY: Of course I was. Wasn't I? Frank! Frank!

FRANCO: Huh?

ROY:	Was I at the wedding?
ANITA:	It's okay, if he said you were there then you were—
ROY:	Was I at the wedding?
FRANCO:	Of course! Whatever makes you happy! Shit—the fish is burning
ROY:	But—
MARIE:	If you weren't high you wouldn't be burning the fucking fish, Franco! Here are the napkins.
ROY:	Louise.
MARIE:	Oh no.
ROY:	Let's go home. I'm tired.
MARIE:	It's dinnertime.
ROY:	I'm not hungry.
MARIE:	Well, I'm starving. I was kind of in the mood for spaghetti but burnt fish'll do.
ROY:	I don't want to stay here anymore.
MARIE:	Feel free to leave anytime.
ROY:	Louise!
MARIE:	Is this what I'm meant to go along with?
ANITA:	Dad…
ROY:	S'il vous plait
MARIE:	Well, since you asked so nicely, no.
ANITA:	Dad, we're just about to sit down to eat the nice dinner you've been helping with
ROY:	I'm sorry, who are you?

ANITA: I'm—it's me.

ROY: Oh. You. Excuse me, if you would, I'm just in the middle of—Louise, can we talk privately for a moment, please?

MARIE: Oh sure. That sounds swell. Let's have a tête-à-tête.

ROY: I'm very uncomfortable here.

MARIE: I know exactly how you feel.

ROY: If this is your way of punishing me, you did it. I feel punished. Now can we go?

MARIE: How am I punishing you?

ROY: Once. I was with her once. Is this what we're doing now? Torturing me with all my indiscretions?

MARIE: My mother did that?

ROY: Don't speak in riddles.

MARIE: Good for her.

ROY: I'm sorry, I'm sorry, I'm sorry, all right? What else do you want me to say?

MARIE: I don't want to do this anymore. Make him stop.

CECE: Roy—you're in the p-p-past

MARIE: Louise is dead.

ROY: You're right here.

MARIE: Fine, then I'm dying.

ROY: No, I don't like to talk about that.

MARIE: That's too bad. Because I have cancer. It's killing me.

ANITA: Oh god, no, please don't—

ROY: No, no, no—I can't—I need to—

MARIE: Chase some tail? Distract yourself?

ROY: No—I need a—

MARIE: Drink? You just gonna drink, Daddy? Like nothing's happening?

CECE: S-s-stop, Marie.

MARIE: You can't run from this. You have to come to terms with it.

ROY: No.

ANITA: Stop it.

MARIE: But today is the day I die. You have to let me go.

ROY: No, I can't—

ANITA: This isn't funny.

MARIE: I'll miss you, my little Banita.

ANITA: Stop.

ROY: Don't leave us.

MARIE: Goodbye.

                ROY holds her. She slides to the floor, dead.

ROY: No. No!

ANITA: Daddy...

ROY: No.

ANITA: Daddy, wait...

                He goes to grieve alone. Pause.

MARIE: That'll buy some time. Should we eat?

They ignore her.

Let's go outside. Yeah? No? Hello? What's going on? Uh… are you not talking to me? That was the worst reenactment of all time, you can't possibly be upset. Oh my god. Sorry, but what was I supposed to do? Just keep on pretending to be her forever…

ROY: (O.S.) *Alouette, gentille alouette, Alouette, je te plumerais!*

MARIE: Oh, no

CECE: He's drunk.

ANITA: Again?

ROY: (O.S.) *Je te plumerais la tête, je te plumerais la tête, et la tête, et la tête —*

CECE: You're too young to know what drunk is.

ANITA: Stupid.

CECE: Yeah.

ROY: (O.S.) *Et la tête — ohhh!*

ANITA: I'm playing the song again.

CECE: You'll wear out the tape.

> *ANITA presses play. INXS "Never Tear us Apart" starts to play.*

It's the last time.

ANITA: *…I—I was standing, you were there, two worlds collided*

CECE: *and they could never ever*

> *ROY storms in.*

ROY: Who's singing!? Who the fuck is singing!? Turn that shit off!

>*ANITA turns it off.*

ANITA: Nobody's singing, Daddy

ROY: You lying to me? You lying right to my face, you little

CECE: It was me, I started it

ROY: I'm not talking to you

CECE: But it was me

ROY: Anita come here

CECE: She shouldn't be in trouble 'cause I was the one who

ROY: Anita, get here now

CECE: Stay, Anita.

ROY: 'Scuse me?

CECE: She didn't do anything wrong.

ROY: No?

CECE: Go drink some water. Sleep it off.

ROY: Oh, okay. Thanks for that.

>*He grabs her head hard.*

CECE: …ah!

ROY: You talking back to me? Huh?

ANITA: Daddy

ROY: Cat got your tongue now, huh?

>*He throws her and her head bangs into the nearest surface. An awful sound.*

Don't ever tell me what to do.

He walks away.

ANITA: *(quietly)* Celeste? Celeste? Are you okay?

FRANCO enters.

FRANCO: How long can it take to get napkins and guacamole?

ROY: I knew I was forgetting something.

MARIE: I gave you the napkins.

ROY: Yes.

CECE: Do you have painkillers? I have a b-bit of a headache.

FRANCO: Sure thing.

MARIE: Try not to crush and snort them on your way back.

FRANCO: Ha ha.

MARIE: I'm not laughing.

He goes.

Should I make lemonade?

ANITA: Do whatever you want to do.

MARIE: Okay.

ANITA: 'Cause you will anyhow.

MARIE: If you're upset just say so.

ANITA: Since it's so obvious, I shouldn't have to.

MARIE: I apologized!

ANITA: When?

CECE: Let's n-not

MARIE: Do you want lemonade, Cece?

CECE: I d-don't c-care.

MARIE: Then I won't. If no one cares, I won't bother

ROY: Louise!

MARIE: Oh, shit.

ROY gives flowers to MARIE.

ROY: These are for you

MARIE: Did you take the flowers out of Cece's arrangement?

ROY: I know I haven't been easy to live with lately... maybe I drink too much—I could cut down a little, I'm sure, but the point is, I do love you, despite what I may or may not have said last night, which you can't even—I mean—whiskey—when I drink whiskey nothing I say is... so... I love you, Petit Chou. And I don't want to sleep on the couch anymore. Can I get back in the bed?

MARIE: Okay, I agreed to let him stay to dinner, not

ANITA: Dad, we're gonna eat dinner now

ROY: I'm not hungry, I'm tired!

MARIE: He's having a drunken memory. He's still drunk

ROY: Damn it, Louise, I'm *apologizing,* can't you see an apology when it's staring you in the face with... daffodils?

CECE: N-narcissus

ANITA: Just accept the apology.

MARIE: Ugh—okay, Daddy, apology accepted.

ROY: When you call me Daddy I feel like you're being sarcastic.

MARIE: Right. Roy. It's okay.

ROY: Give us a kiss.

MARIE: Mwah.

ROY: Not an air kiss. A real kiss.

MARIE: How about later?

ROY: Now.

MARIE: I can't.

ROY: But I apologized. Please. Please. Please.

MARIE: Oh, for the love of—no

ROY kisses MARIE on the mouth.

ROY: Marie?

MARIE wipes off the kiss.

MARIE: Yeah.

ROY: Marie. You look just like… but Louise died, she died, she just died…

ANITA: You put that in his head.

MARIE: It's what happened!

ROY: Oh, no.

ANITA: Dad, Daddy, it's okay.

ROY: Leave me alone. Let go. Let go of me. Let me go. Let go, Banita! Your mother's dead.

He goes. Starts singing.

*Alouette, gentille alouette. Alouette, je te plumerais!
Je te plumerais la tête… je te plu—*

CECE:	His French is so terrible.
MARIE:	Don't be mean.
CECE:	It is, though.
MARIE:	It makes him feel better.
CECE:	He's slaughtering it
MARIE:	It's a song about plucking a bird, so it's kind of appropriate
CECE:	Daddy's little girl
MARIE:	Shut up
CECE:	You are
MARIE:	So what.
CECE:	Banita's too quiet. It's not normal for little girls to be so quiet.

ANITA presses play. "Never Tear Us Apart" plays where it left off.

MARIE:	Not again!
CECE:	*(singing quietly to irritate Marie)* ... I told you, we could fly
MARIE:	Oh my god, don't sing. I hate your voice.
MARIE & CECE:	*'cause we all have wings, but some of us don't know why...*

ROY suddenly approaches, surprising them.

ROY:	Who the fuck sings at a time like this?!
MARIE:	You do, Daddy.
CECE:	Turn it down... he's too drunk to
ROY:	What did you say, Celeste?

MARIE: She didn't say anything

ROY: I'm not talking to you

MARIE: But, Daddy

ROY: Shut it, Marie. I'm not talking to you! What'd you say, Celeste?

CECE: Nothing

ROY: C'mere

MARIE: Dad

ROY: C'mere

CECE: I said you're drunk, which you are, so go cool off somewhere and leave us alone.

ROY: Oh, okay.

          He grabs her by the hair, hard and fast.

CECE: Ah. Dad!

          He throws her and her head cracks against a hard surface. That awful sound again.

          FRANCO enters.

FRANCO: Is ibuprofen okay?!

CECE: S-sure.

ANITA: Dad, I think you forgot something!

ROY: What?

ANITA: The guacamole.

ROY: Yes!

ANITA: It's here.

ROY: Good. Thank you. I made this, you know.

ANITA: I know

                ROY picks up CECE's arrangement.

ROY: What happened to your arrangement, Cece?

MARIE: You took it apart

ROY: I never—why would you say that?

CECE: It's o-k-kay. D-don't w-worry.

ROY: What's wrong? Why are you talking like that?

MARIE: Oh my god.

FRANCO: He doesn't remember?

CECE: It's a n-n-neurogenic s-stutter.

ROY: How did you get it?

CECE: It d-doesn't matter

ROY: When did you get it?

CECE: D-don't w-worry about it.

ROY: I hope it hasn't—that you've been able—that you've still had a good life—I hope.

CECE: …When I c-cut a flower, it's a death. She c-c-can n-never go back t-to the roots she c-c-came from. But then that f-flower becomes the star of a n-new arrangement. The centerpiece of a w-work of art. I ch-changed and it was p-painful but I've m-made my p-p-peace… are y-you c-c-c… crying?

ROY: …a tiny bird died in your mother's hand, she tried to save it but… When she buried it in the ground she said, 'It's okay, now a flower will grow in its place'.

CECE: I r-r-remember.

ROY: Me too.

CECE:	We sh-should eat.

ROY goes.

MARIE:	Yes.
FRANCO:	Wow. That was… wow.
ANITA:	I've got the guacamole.
CECE:	I've got the w-water.
MARIE:	I think that's everything. I'll be right out.

CECE and ANITA go outside.

FRANCO:	Let's eat.
MARIE:	No.
FRANCO:	I'm starving.
MARIE:	You took my father's drugs.
FRANCO:	Oh my god, Marie—I took, like, six milligrams of nothing
MARIE:	Prescription pills with a label of some woman's name who we don't even know—
FRANCO:	We made guacamole. It was very—it was healing
MARIE:	I can't talk to you when you're high—
FRANCO:	High…? …
MARIE:	I'm going outside.
FRANCO:	I'm coming.
MARIE:	No.
FRANCO:	Oh come on, come on, let's have a do-over.
MARIE:	This isn't a game, Franco. What were you even thinking? Were you thinking?

FRANCO: It was a spontaneous kind of

MARIE: Maybe Anita's right; we shouldn't have got married so soon.

FRANCO: What! Anita doesn't know—we're in love, we fell in love

MARIE: We were supposed to wait a year before any—and this is why! Exactly this. Because you're not ready.

FRANCO: I'm not ready? I'm fuckin' ready. I do all the exercises while you roll your eyes. I am *committed*. Even Len says he can see my commitment. I'm getting an A in this marriage and you're barely passing with a C minus.

MARIE: We're not getting graded on our marriage! We're adults!

FRANCO: An A for Amazing. Don't make me tell you what the C's for.

MARIE: Fuck you!

FRANCO: Not that! It's for cocaine. You're just like cocaine. Ask me why.

MARIE: No!

FRANCO: Because you make me feel incredible, like I can do anything.

MARIE: That's

FRANCO: And then you kick drop me to the curb and leave me for dead.

MARIE: It's drop kick

FRANCO: See, I can't do anything right!

MARIE: I need you to go now.

FRANCO: Would it make any difference if we met later? I don't know. Maybe. But you'd probably still be a C. The other C.

MARIE: I need you to get out!

FRANCO: No. This is my place too.

MARIE: I'm going to eat dinner with my family. You better not be here when I come back.

She goes outside, slamming the door.

FRANCO: Fucking bully.

He attempts his energy clearing move.

Fuck it.

He goes to the piano—he plays the chords of "Never Tear Us Apart."

FRANCO: (*mocking*) "I'm just not a fan of that song, I'm just not a fan of that song." *Don't ask me, what you know is true, don't have to tell you…*

He continues singing the song. CECE comes in.

CECE: That was our mother's f-favourite song. I haven't heard it in y-years. She thought Michael Hutchence was t-t-très sexy. It's b-been so long since

MARIE comes in with ANITA.

ANITA: That song.

CECE: I kn-now.

MARIE: Stop playing it, Franco. I told you I hate it.

He doesn't.

CECE: She would have l-liked it. Today of all d-days.

FRANCO:	*I told you we could fly, cause we all have wings but*
ALL:	*some of us don't know why.....*
ROY:	I hate that fucking song!
	FRANCO stops playing.
ANITA:	Hide!
MARIE:	I told you not to play it! Now look what you did!
FRANCO:	I'm sorry
MARIE:	Go! Get out of here!
FRANCO:	But
MARIE:	Go now!
	He goes.
ROY:	Who the fuck sings at a time like this?
ANITA:	Sorry, Daddy
MARIE:	Sorry.
CECE:	… We don't have to apologize
ROY:	What did you say?
CECE:	Nothing, Roy.
ROY:	Roy? You call me Roy now?
CECE:	If you won't act like a father why should we call you one.
MARIE:	Celeste!
ROY:	Is that right?
MARIE:	She doesn't mean it, Daddy.
ROY:	Shut it, Marie.

MARIE: Sorry.

CECE: Stop apologizing.

ROY: You're the one who should apologize.

CECE: Why would I do that?

ROY: Because I told you to.

CECE: Go drink some water. Sober up.

He reaches for her, hard and fast. Grabs her head.

CECE: Ow. Let go!

ROY starts to throw her but ANITA and MARIE hold him hard.

ANITA & MARIE: No, don't!

CECE: Daddy, please.

A moment. ROY looking in CECE's eyes. As though they're suspended.

ROY: …What am I doing? What am I doing…?

And he lets go of her.

Go. Get away from me. Go now.

The girls go quickly out back.

ROY breaks down… alone. A moment.

ANITA and MARIE come back in.

ANITA: Dad? What are you doing?

MARIE: Come on, Dad. We're all outside. We're about to eat.

ROY: Sorry. It's just this day, you know?

MARIE: A lot of memories. We know.

FRANCO comes in.

FRANCO: Hey. Hi. Sorry—I was just walking by and I noticed your piano—who plays?

MARIE: Oh, it's kind of a communal, whoever wants to kind of thing.

FRANCO: Do you mind if I...?

MARIE: We're closed now, actually. But... yeah, sure, go ahead.

He starts to fool around with the chords of "Never Tear Us Apart."

ROY, ANITA and MARIE all stare at him.

FRANCO: ...what?

MARIE: Just... uh...

None of them say.

We're just about to go out back and eat dinner. You can stay and play if you want. Do you want a coffee or anything? Sorry, we don't serve liquor here.

FRANCO: That's perfect because I don't drink.

ROY: Good for you.

MARIE: That's my dad. He's been sober for

ROY: Twenty-three years.

FRANCO: Wow.

MARIE: Roy, this is...?

FRANCO: Franco. Pleasure to meet you, Sir.

ROY: Were you named after...?

FRANCO: No.

ROY: Good.

MARIE: Hi, I'm—

FRANCO: Oh yeah, sorry—I just realized I didn't actually, uh, do the introduction with you and I'd like to properly—whatever, shut up, Franco—maybe I should just start over.

MARIE: ...okay...

FRANCO: Hi. I like your piano.

MARIE: Uh, thanks.

FRANCO: My name's Franco.

MARIE: Marie.

FRANCO: Hi, Marie.

MARIE: Hi, Franco.

ROY: This is my other daughter, Cece

ANITA: Anita

ROY: Woops, Anita

ANITA: Jesus, Dad, your memory

ROY: I know, I know. It's not my fault. I live in a goddamn universe of daughters—this is Anita, Cece's out back

MARIE: Probably wondering what's taking us so long

            CECE walks in. Clearly she has.

            Sorry. We had an unexpected guest. Cece, this is Franco. Franco, Cece.

            CECE smiles.

ROY: You can join us for dinner if you like, Frank.

MARIE: Franco.

FRANCO: Oh no, I couldn't possibly impose

MARIE: We have plenty

ROY: Yes, what are we having again?

ANITA: Spaghetti.

ROY: Of course. Spaghetti. That was my wife's favourite.

FRANCO: It's mine too.

MARIE: Well then…

ANITA: I'll get the parmesan—we have everything we need, right, Cece?

CECE: We…do.

End of play.

In an ideal world we see them sitting and eating.